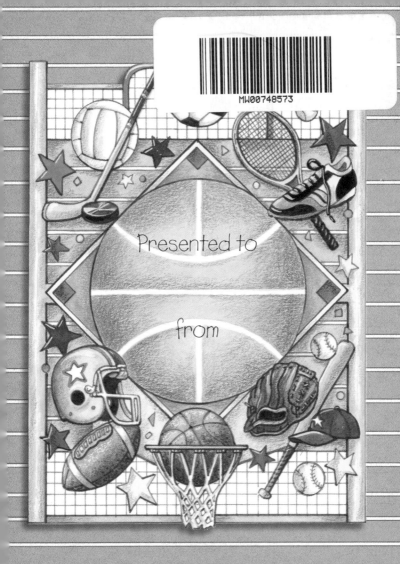

Presented to

from

A son is someone
to celebrate!

I Celebrate You, Son!

Illustrated by Beverly Burge

COUNTRYMAN

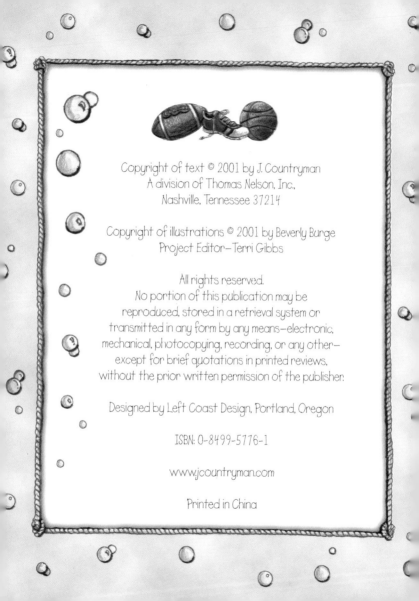

Designed by Left Coast Design, Portland, Oregon

ISBN: 0-8499-5776-1

www.jcountryman.com

Printed in China

Kick that goal!

Make that basket!

Lasso a star!

Everyone likes to feel special.

These are some of the things
that make you special—

_____

_____

_____

_____

_____

_____

_____

_____

_____

_____

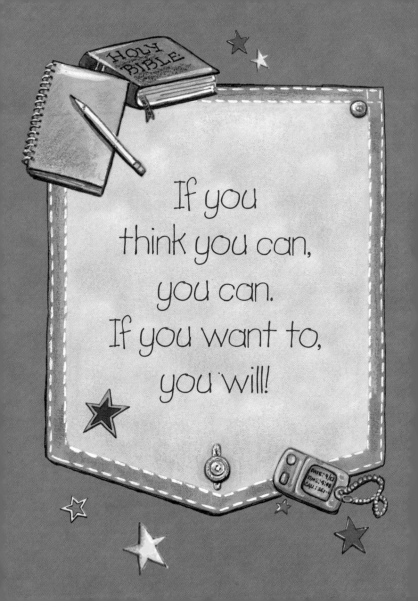

A pocketful of dreams for you.

Having a son like you
makes all the difference.

This is just one way you have made
a difference in my life.

_____

_____

_____

_____

_____

_____

_____

_____

_____

The big news is...

If I could pick
and choose
the one
to be my son,
without a doubt...
yesiree...
I'd choose you!

You deserve
a standing ovation for:

_____

_____

_____

_____

_____

_____

_____

_____

_____

_____

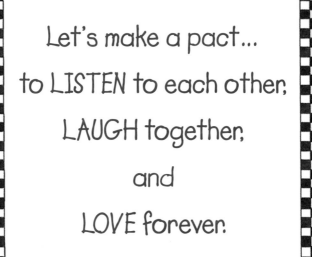

Let's make a pact...
to LISTEN to each other,
LAUGH together,
and
LOVE forever.

Every good
and perfect
gift is
from above.

JAMES 1:17

I'm so glad
God gave
you to me.
That's exactly
the way
it should be!

This is my prayer for you son:

_____

_____

_____

_____

_____

_____

_____

_____

_____

_____

Little
moments
matter
the most.

If I could have
only one wish
come true,
I'd wish the
best in life
for you!

Awesome
adjectives that
describe you—

S _____

O _____

N _____

I celebrate you!

Be wacky
or weird,
clever or cool,
but always
be YOU!